Also by Jonathan Sheppard

SOMEONE SINISTER
BAD STORIES
UNIVERSE UNRAVELING
THE NIGHT I DIED AND OTHER POEMS

JONATHAN SHEPPARD
The Night I Died
and Other Poems

BAD THOUGHTS PUBLISHING COMPANY
LOS ANGELES

BAD THOUGHTS PUBLISHING COMPANY
LOS ANGELES
www.badthoughtspublishing.com

Copyright © 2018 Tyree Jonathan Sheppard
All rights reserved.
ISBN-13: 978-0-692-14972-0
ISBN-10: 0-692-14972-4

CONTENTS

I. RE-DUCE (DEATH), RE-USE (REBIRTH), RE-CYCLE (METEMPSYCHOSIS)   9
II. ONTOLOGICAL CRISIS (Is This A Simulation?)   49
III. ABSOULTION GAINED?   97

THIRTEENTH JUNE 2015

It has been three years since and I cannot help but feel that I am living in a simulation When I woke up in that hospital bed the nurse staring at my nude body under a blanket too small to warm a baby pig I could not help feeling that reality was awkward It felt that I was not in control I was thinking then I would see not see and think Slanted maybe its verity is slanted and reality is not quite what I remember from before that sublime instance that torrid psychotic break because it never could be That selfish circumstance It was wholly selfish I can see that now but in that moment I thought I was being selfless the world and the universe and my family and everyone would be better without me in their lives or the possibility of me being in their lives I did not care that I existed and I would be better off as a fading memory already faded instead of this beacon of self-deprecation sitting here breathing and breathing and breathing a cry baby a big huge crying baby sitting here crying and crying and crying Editing this I feel that I am writing what every person feels who survives a death they called upon Loneliness desolation friendlessness misery woe dejection anger insecurity lack of control addictiveness intense suicidal ideation still indifference extreme happiness extreme gladness extreme laughter and extreme extremity the other side of the spectrum is extreme because you re forcing it maybe you don t know you are you are happy it is not insincere dishonest or deceptive well its only deception is in it lasting or feeling normal or not being extreme or you hoping it will last this time and in the middle of that smile you go blank and then next thing you know you feel bad again and you think about it and it has been awhile since you have felt happy I am still working through dealing with what I did and preventing it from happening again And this simulation is going to help me and has helped me do so Life is not a game there is never ever a metaphor apt to describe what life is and how being no matter what you believe is perception and interpretation I will never blame anything for my thoughts because despite all the psychological evaluations and therapy sessions and my depressing diagnosis I will think them anyway if I was forced to take drugs I would not take them unless I m strapped to a gurney and the drugs are fed into my arm through a hose attached to the thorax of a tick I would not take them why am I depressed am I forced to be depressed I can t help my envy depressed to buy and to be and earn and covet everything I brought it on myself I need to think better but without the delusions I had to think better even if I feel I have no reason I have to think better am I being selective or objective yes even so maybe my mind isn t strong enough Just like it isn t bright enough or strong enough it doesn t have enough strength Is it what I m reading or listening to or watching Am I just going insane in this infinite questions loop the therapist and the psychiatrist told me that they could force me to take the prescription make it a condition of continued ability to stay in my home but they would not they didn t because they trust me what I told them and their diagnoses I believe like I have always believed that I am in control of how I think and that drugs will not influence or be a scapegoat for my thoughts or be allowed to suppress my thoughts If you catch me talking to myself I am just working something out in my mind out loud If what I am saying does not make sense and you cannot understand what is coming from my mind through my vocal chords and lips then maybe it is not for you to understand I would rather people think I am crazy and assume I m depressed or just talking out of my ass and not thinking things through when that is all that I m doing thinking I m crazy is the legal distinction I do not want that stigma attached to me that for some reason my feelings

and my thoughts aren t rational or they are fake or beyond
what is reasonable once you get these mental handicaps
placed upon you nothing you say is taken seriously and you
are always seen as the crazy suicidal person Misunderstanding
is necessary it is a sentiment natural for a poet We relish in
misunderstanding not because we want to but because that is
what interpreting a poem is I think it is I barely understand
the poems that I write that is why I might stop writing them
maybe this is my last poem no more poetry for me I need to
let it go like I almost let go maybe my living means something
else dies not a person not me but the biggest part of me
Trying to navigate this simulation is like navigating a poem
In class when a professor would divulge her interpretation of
a poem in my mind I would think I have no fucking clue
what the fuck she is talking about when songs and films are
interpreted I realize that I am not the only crazy person out
there Naturally that is a flaw in my psychosis I don t want to
write poetry anymore even though I can t help but write it I
m tired of misunderstanding How can the same words illicit
so many responses and feelings How can the same words read
make someone cry make someone laugh and make someone
despondent How can those intense thought filled arduously
written words make you not feel at all Why does the poet
write in the first place Why am I writing I should stop right
here in this moment of all moments This one moment could
be my end It is my end I should stop writing I should let go
Let go of it all Like I let go of myself that night because no
one will ever understand what I m feeling I have written these
words before in the future as right now I know that others
feel exactly like I do and that their feelings are tantamount in
their lives how I feel about what I see and experience and
what I think about knowledge wisdom and potentiality what
about the necessary fragility of life are thoughts that are only
mine just like death is I don t get it what I felt I know that

maybe my almost death was how I gained my new wisdom I survived death and now I have a chance to explore new emotional heights and transcend thought and write short stories and novels maybe I ll finally write that script and write more things that are perfect for misinterpretation and misunderstanding I still remember vividly in all that chaos that I was ready to go I was ready to not be here I knew I understood that everyone would be better if I was not here The platitudes of depression aside I did not know I was suicidal despite everything I wrote and all the clues and all the signs I ignored those signs like all the signs of a school shooter after a school shooter shoots up a school I am the realization afterwards that all of the signs were ignored again and again shot after shot explosion and life and students and teachers all gone for ignoring I was a small town ignoring that they are harboring and enabling destruction I am the Principal Vice Principal and the Chancellor and Dean and all the doctorate and bachelor candidates alike Trying our best to keep from thoughts of death because achieving what we should seems worth it because life is milestones achievements and ability not chaos discord misrule entropy and destruction bedlam untidiness derangement clutter and mistake Life is not knowledge or its absence Life is not the ability to take life away give life or nurture life Life is how each breath is decided Breathing is not involuntary We can end each breath after each breath We can choose to decide that breathing is not an option because we shot and killed twenty-five people in a high school or because it has been decided that no one cares if you kill you or not if you exist or not There is no selfishness or selflessness it is just you deciding if you want to exist or not and everything and everyone surrounding your choice is just auxiliary they are ancillary because you know that you alone decide value and importance And in that moment death is of the upmost importance I am sorry I forgot to explain why I feel that I am living in a simulation why I am living in a world where every choice I make every thought I have is controlled I am not acting at all A chip underneath one of the scars where that blade carved up my arm is controlling me something that was imbedded into my arm on the thread of one of those hundreds of stitches is controlling my reality The blood needed used to replace those four pints I loss was infused with a substance that insured that my life was to be lived like a robot When a friend or anyone says anything to me they are foreshadowing every miniscule aspect of the life that I was used to living I think of turtles and now I see a turtle and then for some reason my day is surrounded by turtles and how I need to develop a defense system like a turtle but then my lady wants turtle soup and my son watches Ninja Turtles after never caring about turtles ever Now I have to become a protector of turtles a conservationist to protect all turtles I hear bells then I get texts about eating bell peppers I think of the number 19 then I see it everywhere and every number I see is divisible by 19 One and one, two and two, six and seven and eight and infinity I know what you are going to think and say because this simulation ensures that I do this simulation tells my thoughts to forget that there are psychological explanations for your feeling that things are more than a string of infinite coincidences that chaos is ordered and fate is how the universe is controlled and karma is real you drive everyone else crazy so you are really crazy the simulation tells me that I m on a path created for me so think and everything in your path will form to those thoughts and form I often ramble and forget I am in this simulation I get to control certain aspects of my life like my diet and my temperament and my diet is getting better and so is my temperament but then again maybe it is the programming maybe the blood donated to me was vegan blood maybe cannibal blood maybe the blood of a killer or a veterinarian Is it my blood controlling my simulation or because I choose not to be fat or angry I remember being told that your death is not going to be easy I remember being told that I do not know who told me that my death was going to be easy but killing me is going to be hard and you have failed this time if it was a random voice or recording I just know that I heard it The runners of this simulation are ensuring that I live Not for my own well being but because they want to prove that life is worth it to them My entire time alive which is only the three years since I died I am a toddler a cry baby I have only been proving that life is worth living because I barely know that I am alive And I prove that life is worth living just by professing it I can t prove it by any measure of worth I just know that it is It is necessary for my survival the horrible conditions and the purely awful and evil nature of the world This is not a simulation because there is no truer world this is not the Matrix and it s simplicity There is no alternate world or reality or some background information parallel universes video games social media posts infinite amount of dimensions heavens or hells all the excuses to escape from what we all know we need to escape from And even still three years later although I m not going to commemorate this date ever again just explaining how I m trying to even begin to feel is just selfish I still haven t quantified or even acknowledged how my family feels my lover and my son not too many people know they don t know I do not need people to care I don t even know why I m doing this this goddamn simulation I ve been trying to get over it myself Trying to figure out what s true and what s real And what s being purposely placed in front of me How do I know what to choose How do I feel when I wake up today How did I feel when I woke up later Why did I feel like waking up today Why do I just want to lie here tomorrow There is nothing wrong with what I am feeling There is something wrong with killing myself I don t know if that s how I will go All I know is that I m going to live until I figure out if this is a simulation or not Hopefully it takes forever

RE-DUCE (DEATH), RE-USE (RE-BIRTH), RE-CYCLE (METEMPSYCHOSIS)

Ere the birth of my life, if I wished it or no
No question was asked me--it could not be so!
If the life was the question, a thing sent to try
And to live on be YES; what can NO be? to die.

NATURE'S ANSWER

Is't returned, as 'twas sent? Is't no worse for the wear?
Think first, what you ARE! Call to mind what you WERE!
I gave you innocence, I gave you hope,
Gave health, and genius, and an ample scope,
Return you me guilt, lethargy, despair?
Make out the invent'ry ; inspect, compare!
Then die--if die you dare![1]

---

[1] "The Suicide's Argument" a poem by Samuel Taylor Coleridge, Coleridge was a late 18th century early 19th century British poet. From *The Complete Poems*, by Samuel Taylor Coleridge, Penguin Books, 1997. Coleridge wrote in *Lecture and Notes on William Shakespeare* "Follow the wandering spirit of poetry through its various metempsychoses, and consequent metamorphoses."

THE NIGHT I DIED

I did not plan on dying
Most people never plan to die
Even when you know
Maybe even when you are told
You do not know that you are going…
Even sadder…
You do not know that you want to
This is not your climax
This is your end
Your climax was something random
Like eating a chili dog in your hometown
Or an eerily and unusually cold Los Angeles Spring night
My right hand cut through the graveyard
My right hand decapitated the devil
A heart transmitting the hate of darkness
The damage done
Head half gone
The devil drops the ticket
Picks up the knife and goes after your new home
And how you should lose it and leave
Right underneath death
Here and here, cut here
You talk but ramblings possess you
Incoherently you lie
Moments from death you keep lying
Because you are sure that you are dying
Or at least you would not mind if you did
Because that is something you will do, surely
So it does not matter if you tell the truth
It does not matter if you are standing or lying
In your own blood
Selfishness makes you figure that your life

Means only something to you
What I think in my mind about myself
Is not all that is important
Consciously, I covet a fight that you will soon lose too
Life drains from you
You call the only person who will ever care
You apologize for being
You apologize for loving
You apologize for what you drank
You apologize for not believing
You apologize for the eyes that saw
You apologize for the ears that heard
You apologize for finally making a decision for yourself
You apologize then realize…
That maybe you should not make decisions
But it is too late
You are on a gurney almost unconscious
Damage to your kidneys and psyche
Your decision was made
And you did not survive, like you thought
And you died…
I died
I didn't want to be around
I don't want to love or hate or feel
I don't want to be able to drink or eat
I wish I couldn't see or hear
Maybe I wish I didn't wish those things
Maybe, again, I'm sorry…
The night I died
I truly realized
That I'm already dead
I have been dead for a while
And I'm going to keep being dead
Crazy I am

The first thought, of course
Ask your question so I can fit the profile of your questions
Tell me that I'm insane
It is 2009, it is 2005
I was born this very moment, right here and right now
I'm the insane person?
Because I know what's going to happen?
And understand that end?
All that I'll ever do is die
The selflessness of this display will never equal the need
For comfort
Again, I died; you are comfortable
I am dead, I am comfortable

EMPTY ROOM

Bargain with me
I am here, right here
I've stood right here before
I know that I have, I feel like I have
With the same people in the same room
Where I've always stood
Look at me like I shouldn't be here
I know that I shouldn't be here
This room should be empty
Except for them
And thoughts of me being gone

APOCRYPHA

My work is genuine
So there is no need for doubt
Most of it is exaggerated fiction
I originally thought I was writing with true feeling
True knowledge, chaotic structure, but true
That's how I felt
They were actually written
And I preached those feelings and feeling that way
Or that way, or like that
Honest to my deepest, darkest, truest mind and heart
Those words written were true then
They had to have been
No matter I told my truth
And it ruled my universe
It won't anymore
It will be forged
It will be contrived
But it won't be lies
I will it to be gospel
You will too

EASY WAY OUT

The easy way out is what I tried to choose
Kill me now!
An easy plan and not a random act
Softly, you haven't made that choice...
Or thought about it yet or often
Maybe you haven't because it is the "easy" thing to do
And you're only into doing things difficultly
That's why I tried to take the easy way out
I wanted to give up on doing difficult things
I must be an idiot
Because I tried to take the easy way out, and failed
Now I have to live life hardened

THE DESCENT OF THE DISTRAIT DYAD

I am not two people that is true
I am one body, one hue
One mind
That thinks in concert with one time
Skeptics there are many of those
Them and the doubters I oppose
Some of my actions may have been done in two
As some actions did to do
That perception does not call me aloof
I am one person, why do you need proof?
I am one person too
Why are you in my head?
Or why are you wondering what's in there
What's in here?
I have a brain just like you
I am not blind, I can see and smell
Touch and know and ask and insult
This is an insult! I am one person!
He is... I mean I am too

CREATIVE CONVERTING…

Change is good, that's supposed to be believed
Growth is great and growth is all life actually achieves
Intelligence, fight, family, bones and body's girth
Burgeoning self and economic worth
Even if you lose all you have received
That change is still as moral as your birth

I AM HERE FOR A REASON

I almost left this page blank
But I have my son to thank
How can I tell him that I don't see a reason
In not living along side him for dozens of seasons
I am here to give him all he wants and needs
And to wipe his tears and kiss his scraped knees
I am here to watch him grow as tall as the trees
And to help his mind expand helplessly
Despite the universe's guile
I only want to see him smile
Wholly I fear
That he would smile less if I weren't here

FRAIL MIND

Those thoughts I once thought were feeble
Are now prominent and own me
What are those thoughts?
Thoughts of life and how it leaves, how it is fleeting
Thoughts of death and how it is imminent
My regard was for my simple soul
And how I knew I shouldn't have a soul
How my breath should not have been
I wanted to appease the inevitable
I wanted to forget how I thought
Often still, I want to forget how I think
All of these causes and thoughts of worth
How all of us billions are worth something
When truly we're cockroaches
In an infested house with a two o'clock appointment
With the exterminator
Truly, I don't want to break
I want to continue to write poems no one reads
I want to continue to be the only person who cares about me
But I'm falling apart
I'm fragile like the vase falling from twenty stories
I'm fragile like the sage telling twenty honest stories
The mind is frail, my mind is frail, life is frail
I'm sorry that it crippled me
I'm sorry that I'm not as strong as I should be

YOU CAN'T FORGET: CAUSAL DEPENDENCE

Memory is scary
A penny on the ground
Reminds me of times spent with my Grandpa
As he picked up one at the bus stop
He told me that 99 more of those makes one dollar
That's why a penny lost
Is a penny closer to being broke
$999,999,999.99
One penny more is that much more worth
Now, I pick up every penny I see abandoned
Put it in my pocket
Then later into my penny jar
And think about my Grandpa as I close the lid
Priceless were those times we spent together
Memory isn't scary now
Because those memories make me feel richer

AN EXISTENTIALIST'S RATIONALE

There is no synonym or other known understanding
Because free will is too demanding
The weather, traffic, or the free will of other beings
Does not and will not cause my responsibility to go fleeing
The will I exhibited before those causes came
I still stand firmly with my choice's shame
Nothingness isn't absurd
And neither are the ethics defined as disturbed
It guides the angst in all of my choices
I am free to not listen to the voices
Here I am still, breathing healthy breaths
Never rationalizing what becomes of my will
For all of my steps are guided
By how I tell myself to feel

SELF-MEDICATE

The social worker, the therapist and the psychiatrist are worried
They fear that I will self-medicate
They don't want me to deal with life's flurries
With alcohol, weed, cocaine with illegal drugs or bad habits
But they do want to give me their drugs in a hurry
For my fragile temperament and glum disposition
Their medicine is the only medicine that should cure my lethargy
Do not self-medicate they insist
Again, "take our drugs in a hurry!"
Maybe they'll harm me and maybe they won't
"Your life will be better lived if because of our drugs you're buried"

TRUE BEAUTY

A child wept
A mother cried
A father shed a tear
The family was sad
It was beautiful
Because soon
They'd smile

I CREATE AS I SPEAK

I am not speaking
I am writing
But maybe one day I will say these words
And they will live
They will be heard and hated
Unwittingly I will admit by my actions
That what I feel as I read this aloud to myself
Has created something unexplainable in me
I will submit to the words I hear
Hopefully, what I write and then say creates love and life
Not doubt and death
Abracadabra

YOUR EYES ARE CLOSED, YOU MUST BE SLEEPING

When you type on your phone
You must be texting
You're writing a poem you say? Make that poem known!
When you need time to yourself
You must hate being around people
You need space you say? Here is space and it's wealth!
When your eyes are closed
You must be sleeping
You're thinking you say? About what I suppose?
When your eyes are closed and you're not asleep
Please open them for my comfort
Don't make me weep
Think with your eyes open for me

THE VEIL OF THE MACABRE

Here comes death again
Ready to pull out your eyes
And blow out your brains
Death will use a friend
To bury you alive
To make you lame
An axe murderer or chainsaw wielder
Just like the 2,000 stab wounds
Or mangled hands wrapped around your neck
Are the builders of your tomb
And your life after death
So no matter how your consciousness ends
Even gruesomely unexpected
Take solace in the truth
That death's sins
Do not mean that you'll be resurrected
Because you've died better than others do

ADJUSTMENT DISORDER

And that's my diagnosis
Don't misunderstand me
That's the diagnosis I was given
They thought that I might have been depressed
So that moment of undeniable psychosis
Was fleeting and had my mind deceived
It wasn't a prolonged episode that would govern my intentions
Work, family, anxiety, writing and all those other stresses
I am having trouble adjusting to
I can yell and scream or I can stay silent
But still the adjustments I am struggling to make drag
And no one I know cares about my knowledge
Maybe knowledge is nothing without wisdom's do
So to ask for care is to be too reliant
Upon my life and how it lags
And also to rely upon the pledge
That someone just one actually loves you
I know she only cares about me, that's all
She also only cares about how she feels
And not fixing what is wrong with her
She is perfect and I am flawed, that's true
So every cuts call
She easily repeals
For adjustment has nothing to do with her
She is always right
And her anger and her temper and her everything
Must always be appeased and adjusted to
It doesn't matter how I feel or what I say
And no matter what I decide with all my might
There is nothing I could think or sing
I just have to do

Whatever she feels I should play
Although I know that adjusting to her will
Means that me I will kill

DARK ENERGY

I have noticed that a lot of people think
That things should be a certain way
There is a truth that permeates through humanity, that links

All of mankind to a very strict behavioral display
But also there is this mysterious and awkward feeling that stinks
It represents truth and its decay

It causes some of humanity to act passed sanity's brink
The happiness and good that should be felt by mankind everyday
Is bastardized, exploited and in some souls extinct

How can we as humans accept this dismay?
We must fight against those who skate outside the universe's moral rink
The universe in all its vastness should only relay

Comfort, beauty, and a pure motive is all we should drink
From disturbed inclinations, impulsions, and their necessity we must stray
Every person on the planet must believe what the moralists think

I have a feeling that what I know is for truth's sake
But it cannot be heeded to because I misunderstand human nature's say
Maybe the truth and morality are not always the only take
Surely, we are a dark energy's prey

LOVE ABUSE

Something that feels so good must be good to everyone
Sharing is caring and to hold this feeling in
Is only a detriment to its worth
Love can only mean something if shared
I love you, I love me, I love him and her
I LOVE EVERYONE AND EVERYTHING
Love, love, love, love, love

What bothers me most is that the word almost has no value now
The word has been inflated and made nearly worthless
"I love this restaurant and I absolutely love its décor"
"I love this season of [enter TV show here]" "I love this movie"
"I love my car and my house" "I love my apartment"
"I love this book"
I LOVE EVERYONE AND EVERYTHING

I love you, I love me, I love him and her
Love can only mean something if shared
Sharing is caring and to hold this feeling in
Is only a detriment to its worth
Maybe love's meaning changes to what the word is applied
I'm sure some people believe that
But to me it all sounds the same

A good meal and love for child can be equated
Maybe they're intertwined causally
In fact, maybe love is this universal experience that cannot be exploited
Maybe love is a word we should use much much more
Love is special

That's why everyone and everything should have it
That's the only reason I hate it
Love is a word abused
And is used so often that it can't be felt
We need to use it much much less
So we can feel it and act upon it much much more

FIGHT VIDEO

Violence one more time on camera
A conflict between two humans that had to be settled with physicality
I feel sorry for the cameraperson and the crowd
I feel sorry for the website that will accept its upload
I feel sorry for the winner
One day that winner will be a loser
Just like we all are at sometime
And there will be a camera there to ridicule
Millions of views
But when the camera turns off
Someone will grab a weapon, a gun
And get the last laugh
With only one view
That knock out
Won't end the conflict that turned to death
This tragedy will be replayed throughout the annals of time

OIL ON CANVAS

Crossing that slick bridge
With oil piled on thick
I thought I'd slipped past the jagged ridge
But I then looked at my clothing ragged
My eyes tried to stop my mind
But it was too late to say bye
I fell into the meadow to find
That I had nothing to do
But stare and stare and stare
I followed stroke after stroke after stroke damned
The clocks around me broke
Aimless, trapped in a sea

CONFIRMATION BIAS

Why can't you understand that your opinion is simply a telescope
Your opinion is a microscope
You dig and dig and search and look for pain
That only confirms your pain and why you're in pain
Powerful instruments of discovery are abused
Because you want to be abused
The world is horrible
The universe is horrible
Because of what you see in that lens
It becomes even smaller because of what you see in that lens
You know what you're looking for
And validation is what you're looking for
So even though you're curious and look everywhere
You look there, you look here, you look beyond, near, everywhere!
Did you find what you were looking for?
Can you explain what happened before?
You're looking to magnify what you believe you see
Witness a defect then condemn every organism you see
You feel slighted
You truly feel slighted
But how you feel isn't what is
How you feel isn't how everything is
So keep looking, look
Find what you're looking for, look
Keep focus
Truly focus
I know what you've found
The world and the universe is against you is what you've found

SCHOOLED IN EDUCATION

You thought you were smart
In fact, you know more than most
You have your degree
Honestly, you are smarter
You followed the rules
You will make more when you learn
How to go to school
What the schooled often don't learn
Is education always begins
You will never be the smartest
If you think you'll ever be done
Being educated

YOU STILL DON'T KNOW ME

You're mad again; rather, you're irritated
I breathed
Yep, you're tired of me breathing around you
I'm growing
I don't act on emotion anymore
I'm all about my doomed company
I'm all about not reacting in every single moment
I'm all about not wanting to kill myself because I know
That you truly don't want me
I'm all about focusing on bettering myself
Which will better my business and my family
I once was told that family does things together
That's true!
But what else does family do?
They support each other!
They understand each other!
Family doesn't just care if the child eats
But if the father eats
Family cares about each others mental and physical well being
And you don't care about anything about me
All you care about is how I do whatever you want
Because you're looking for any reason to find another
I'm at my breaking point
I don't give a fuck!
I'll become homeless
I'll pay child support
I'll do anything to not feel how you make me feel
I'm not going to die because you can't heal
You don't want to better yourself
You haven't learned any lesson from my near death
You're even more selfish now
I feel like a goddamn fool and a loser

Because I'm just here to take your abuse
Family isn't reactionary
Family isn't so quick to discard
You want me to be apart of the family
But you want me out the house every Sunday
You want me out of the family!
I'm not needed
I'm disposable
You don't care about me being in this family
You're all that matters
That's why you still don't know me
Or maybe you do
And that's why you don't love me

THE COMMEMORATION OF MY FAKE DEATH

Sunrise 11/19/1985, Sunset 06/13/2015 to Present

Deep lacerations on both my arms
Four pints of blood gone
I don't know who I charmed
But I was alive and death I had conned

Today I feel like I did a year ago, that night
In and out of consciousness feeling like a ghost
"Don't fucking touch me, let me die, that's my right."
I remember rambling to the police about intelligence, stupidly, I did boast

How idiotic when I was dumb enough to try and leave my lady and my son
"Stay with me Jonathan, what were you drinking tonight?"
"Wild Turkey and shots of... I'm done"
"Stay with me Jonathan... Hey [...] isn't Wild Turkey what you like?"

Fire fighters are heroes, I suppose
Suicide watch felt lonely
"Do you want some underwear? You don't have to be exposed."
"Why are you here? It should be me only."

"What year are we in?" "2009"
"Do you know where you are?" "Yes, in high school."
They expected a man handcuffed to a hospital bed to be fine
"What year are we in?" "2015" "You're not insane or a fool."

My lady brought me food everyday
The hospital food I couldn't eat
It had to be food served in hell everyday
From her love and care I could not retreat

"We're going to have to keep you in the hospital for seven more days
Maybe longer..."
"I understand what I did. I won't do it again. I was in a sullen daze."
"Well, we must ensure that you're not a danger... that you're stronger."

Door off hinges
I arrive home and immediately grab my power drill
I fix the door so burglars can't binge
My son walks up the steps and smiles in shock to see that his father is real

I died a year ago, exactly one year
And lived to tell how I survived death
So death I no longer fear
I'm going to live forever for my son's breath

TOMORROW, TOMORROW, I HATE YOU TOMORROW

Tomorrow, tomorrow I don't hate you for your potential gloom
Tomorrow, tomorrow I don't hate you for your cloudless skies
Tomorrow I won't hate even if tomorrow is the day they engrave my tomb
And tomorrow the maggots devour my eyes

Uncertainty should not be hated
Neither should darkness or light
What I hate most about tomorrow is what is baited
That it is another chance to do, another chance to be right

Tomorrow, tomorrow you're just another excuse
I lie awake 48 hours, I lie awake 72 hours, I may never sleep
Tomorrow I want to avoid you; today's work must produce
Tomorrow you can wait; tomorrow I don't want to meet

Tomorrow, tomorrow I don't hate you for your potential gloom
Tomorrow, tomorrow I don't hate you for your cloudless skies
Tomorrow I won't hate even if tomorrow is the day they engrave my tomb
And tomorrow the maggots devour my eyes

ILLUSION OF CHOICE

Deciding is hard
I don't know what's best to choose
Is this the only choice?
Are you sure?
Then I refuse
Well...
I can't do that
I have to decide
I choose the only choice

CLARITY

I have never wanted to be clairvoyant
To see what will happen
To know that it will happen
Sometime, somewhere
I don't believe in clairvoyance
The windshield is too dirty
The window is boarded up
My mind is cloudy
And can only see the past
That's how I know what I'll see
Because of what I've been through
That's how I know what I won't see
Because of what I will go through

THE FIRST LAW OF THERMODYNAMICS

I am obsessed with death and the energy and its thought processes
Those tend to lend themselves to my fragile mortality
I understand what that means
That most people, most beings' energy won't align to mine
They will avoid me like they avoid dealing with death and sadness

Like they circumvent confronting madness
I'm tired of people refusing pain but accepting time
And not understanding that comfort is not what it seems
You can isolate the smiley faces, flowers, rainbows, and gumdrops as practicality
But you will realize that the energy that causes darkness which pain obsesses

Is not different, a simple avoidance, or some inane effigy
That energy you feel that you always want to avoid
You hope to destroy that power that causes your frowns
Pain is something you cannot bare so you wish it dead
All of your perceived negativity, dissipates, evaporates it absconds

Happiness, a stoic well being, productivity and positivity are the forces that you find fond
The energies that you find least evident in my head
You never think that maybe this dark, deathly energy has been around
That it occupies a much-needed void
That it always has and that it will always be

Those dark times that you thought had left
Because good times came and destroyed them all
Were a farce, ignorance and its inability to comfort
Death and loathing, loathing and death, death and loathing
Forget about it; disremember it because it doesn't have to exist

Your type is whom I cannot resist
Those who go aimlessly poaching
For a universe that is absent of death and loathing, where sorrow is encumbered
But you cannot disavowal that bad thoughts survive, wrought from energy banal
An energy that always survives death over and over again it survives death

NO LIVES MATTER

No one deserves to live
No one deserves to die
There isn't a time perfect
Or a time too imperfect
There isn't a place serene
There isn't a way standard
We only care because we're here
If we were gone
Like who our tears find fond
We wouldn't care either
We die
Maybe too soon, maybe not soon enough
Maybe it should have been natural causes
Maybe we should prevent death from happening a certain way
It doesn't matter
Immortality!
We're gonna die
Someone took my life
Someone owned theirs
I am not because someone told me I was
I do not have matter for validation
No space can I live
I don't mean to matter to you

ONTOLOGICAL CRISIS (IS THIS A SIMULATION?)

"The destructive character sees nothing permanent. But for this very reason he sees ways everywhere. Where others encounter walls or mountains, there, too, he sees a way. But because he sees a way everywhere, he has to clear things from it everywhere. Not always by brute force, sometimes by the most refined. Because he sees ways everywhere, he always stands at a crossroads. No moment can know what the next will bring. What exists he reduces to rubble – not for the sake of rubble, but for that of the way leading through it.

The destructive character lives from the feeling not that life is worth living, but that suicide is not worth the trouble."[2]

---

[2] Walter Benjamin's *"The Destructive Character."* Walter Benjamin was a Jewish philosopher and essayist; he fled Nazi Germany in 1932. Benjamin killed himself in 1940. Text originally published in the *Frankfurter Zeitung* in 1931.

ACTING ON BAD THOUGHTS

I obviously do not mind having bad thoughts
I laugh at weird deaths
I didn't cause that weird death but I wish I had
Oh how I thought about killing her myself, now I can rest
Random motorcyclist thank you for ridding my world of her
All of the bad thoughts that I obsessed
The thoughts I refused to let become action
Have left

THE CRIMINAL ENTERPRISE WE REFUSE TO ACKNOWLEDGE ON PURPOSE

The nobility of this criminal enterprise is never questioned
Its righteous, morality, could be anything but a dream
The leaders of this sinister syndicate always tout its good ambitions
But can never manifest what the words mean
Subservient to this grand ideal
Its actions we never appeal

Serve and preach, preach and serve
"The United States' intentions are always on the side of good"
I am unnerved
By the deceit of intentions and how their actions are falsehoods
It's too difficult to hope
It is easy to cope

My luxury, as minimal as it is
Is something I will cherish with my life
Something I refuse, something I will fight... not to relinquish
How can I honor what is right
When the only model I have to gain influence from, to copy
Is wrong and a hypocrite and abusive and exploitive and sloppy?

We are the citizens of the United States of America, and we're criminals!

SOCIAL CONTRACT

We agree to agree
Do not let any one fail you in their assessment
If you decide to live around here
You've decided to subject yourself
To how we do things around here

UNATTAINABLE IDEALISM

Someday we're going to realize
That we should not strive for what we idealize
We need to understand that justice is a myth
And dreams of equality leave everyone pissed
I understand that it may be difficult to let go
Of what you aspire to relish, to know
But these ideals have never been shown
These ideals no one has ever known
Liberty is attached to the chains of money
And happiness is an infinite want for dummies
Our idealism is not how things should be
Because our collective idealism has never been reality

DEATH IS FOR THE LIVING

When I die again
Live like I was still around
Your tears won't help me

I AM NOT READY

I am not ready
I need time to adjust to what just happened
Now this is happening...
As this is happening, something is being prepared to happen soon
How many things are happening?
That many?
One after another after another and then at the same time?
I am not ready
Innovation or progress I do not mean to restrict or dampen
But calm the hell down!
Better doesn't mean better
Why can't we trade better for greater?
Is it profit and attention span and impulse,
And how they are simply exploited?
I am not ready
I get a notification every time I have to piss
I've walked 800,000 steps today
Find a toilet... turn here
I am going to beat 800,000 steps today
I don't even know why I am tracking that
I didn't set that!
I have taken only ten trillion breaths today
And the average is much much higher
I will be ready
We must be rushed
I am ready

RADICAL CHIC

It is trendy to
Be hardcore and real edgy
Rebels, birthed uncool

ANOTHER YEAR DOWN

I made it!
Another resolution I get to make
I was bullshitting everyday last year
Today is where I make things right
Another year down, I have survived
I can continue to be who I am
You won't change me

YOU THINK THIS IS HOW I SHOULD LIVE MY LIFE?

So this is how I should live my life
Go to work come home and go to sleep
Do not stay up hours writing shit no one is going to read?
Especially you
You want me to hide how unsupportive you are
But I will not anymore
You hate that I'm a writer and I'm compelled to do something
Without being paid for it
Give up! Rely upon being a wage slave to feed my family
That's what you want
Hopefully, my wage will be passed along to our son
For your comfort I should sleep next to you at night
I shouldn't continue to work and write and write and write
I know it is futile
You know it is too that's why you want me to stop
You do not want me to create or express myself
I should just work a perfect job with perfect hours
Hours that fit our schedule
I should just do that
And not write at all
I need to give up on writing and let it go
I need to give up on expression and let it go
Well I'm not
I'll kill myself before I do
I will not live my life like you want me to

ISOLATION

I was alone for most of Thanksgiving Day, cooking
I was alone for most of Christmas Eve
I was alone for most of Christmas Day
I was alone for New Year's Eve
I was alone for New Year's Day
Holidays are made up days
So there isn't any necessity to be around family
But I was alone
I'm still alone
I don't want to be here

WHO TOWS THE LAST TOW TRUCK?

Valiant tow truck driver
Stranded because of a broken axel
Today the tow truck driver
Towed many tow trucks
All of them is the number actual
All but the one tow truck that is stuck

I SUPPORT OUR PRESIDENT

I support our president
Truly, I hoped he would win
Despite believing a loss was evident
I always believed in him

What he has said and will say is captivating
I cannot wait to hear what he says, what he thinks
When he won, I was elated holy, by what he was cultivating
A society, a nation on destruction's cold, indiscriminate brink

He is only saying what our nation has been doing forever
We have to reckon with our privilege around the globe
Our vanity, our impulse to feel good, to buy, to exploit, and how those flaws we cover
I support our president because the history, the darkness we hide; he shows

Let him lie, let him deny you and us, your community, our people
Let him lead this country down the path of its inevitable destitution
Let him be honest about what has always made this country full
Let our president destroy this nation; for the world's retribution

ABSOLUTION MOMENTARILY

Left, left, left, right, left
March… SCREAM! for equality
Equal to whom though?

HUMAN ERROR

Self-driving cars will soon be here
Other than repairs, these cars will be perfect
Everyone will be given one
They will exceed the speeds in which the law adheres
The driver reclined, watching a film, texting her boyfriend, he won't be nervous
It has been proven that self-driving cars don't crash
The car companies have done many tests, tons
They are solar powered, battery battered, fossil fuel absent, their bodies will last

The sound system links to your smartphone, it recognizes your phone's serial number
Actually, the car's computer system, and every screen act as your phone
Humanity will soon be driving smart cars, predictive and intuitive
No U-turns, no bad directions that make you wander
All alone?
Your car will also converse with you
Honestly and truthfully, everything you say no matter how ruinous
You won't rue

Despite the car being built perfectly strong
It will still register your complaints
It does not matter how you complain or what they are
The car will know what's wrong
Errors aren't, they ain't
Perfection is needed and at stake
Perfection is this car
Damn, I cannot believe they forgot brakes

COMMUNITY IS DEAD

Community is dead
We do not want to know our neighbors
Smile and exchange inane pleasantries
Hypnotized by the grin and the wave

That is what we save
A grin and wave are all we need
To decide that who we live close to aren't sore
Community is dead

All alone he lived
He went to work he said "Hello!"
He grilled in his backyard and showed his teeth when you asked
You just knew he was a nice man

He helped you take out your trashcans
He helped you with any great or menial task
There was always a smile and a "hello"
He had a home, no wife, and no kids

You knew him as a nice man
He was more than willing to help the community
And now the community is dead
Because the community understood what a smile meant

Smiles mean goodness and happiness are sent
What most have said
Is that this was a wonderful and safe community
He killed them all! Every member of this community damned

You never know your neighbors
To the left and right of you, adjacent and far
It is clear that you definitely did not know that neighbor's core
We found all those dead bodies in his yard

THE BATTLE FOR CALIFORNIA

There is no way the United States let's us go
Of course Canada wants us
Mexico used to be us and still should be
What you all need to know
Is that if you want us
We have to control all policy

NOT EVERYONE CAN READ

In these trying times
One of our greatest missteps is assuming intelligence
Just because you are engaging in an argument, a sit down, or civil conversation
That does not mean that that person or you will understand it

Some people will understand the terms you define
Some will ignore them with the most ignorant negligence
You are not equal to everyone you're facin'
There are varying degrees of wit

You cannot count on everyone's great ability to comprehend
You cannot count on everyone being idiotic
Your definitions and understanding are not the truth or the end
What is the topic?

Explain all you want
They're not going to get it or understand
Give them links and sources, be considerate
They are trying to fight anger and its sensation, frustration

Please forgive my taunt
I cannot believe it is taking this long, damn!
I think you're illiterate
I will help you understand, I have patience

Some people will understand the terms you define
Some will ignore them with the most ignorant negligence
You are not equal to everyone you're facin'
There are varying degrees of wit

THE TIMES THEY HAVEN'T CHANGED IN A LONG TIME

This age is static
Nothing has been changed ever!
Just renamed, defined

A BURDEN

A burden
Lovely a burden
Cancel that work
Ugly is that burden

Ugly is a life certain
Cancelled because of worth
Lovely a burden
Which is my burden

THE MEDIA IS A JOKE

Knock! Knock!
A reporter here
Here to ask you a couple questions
Please answer in jest
I'm not going to answer the door for you
Humiliate me, you will not
You may scare me for it is the truth I fear
My bosses will not let me pursue lessons
Outside of the youth's ignorant and idiotic behest
I was lied to

Knock! Knock!
It's the same reporter wondering; what do you want?
Do you want neutral unbiased news coverage for yourself
And all you care about; or is it for no one?
Everyone deserves equal ink
The bad joke that no one wants to stop
Is that modern media is nothing but fonts and taunts
And loud talkers, unfunny buffoons, braggadocios in how themselves
Are a farce, aren't funny, or fun
That makes even me, the reporter, unthink

I am mad because you haven't
Been amazed by what I thought was funny or smart or stunning
Since laughter's advent
There hasn't been a joke more cunning

BUILD AND EAT

Knee deep in mud and dirt he built
Famished and starving he built
He built until the skyline changed
She was deranged
She ate too well too often
She ate him as she built his coffin

I HAVE A QUEER DOG

My dog humps the legs of my girlfriend's best girlfriend
My dog humps the legs of my girlfriend's best girlfriend's boyfriend
He humps stuffed animals and my son's action figures
He humps the side of the couch
He humps the air, oh he loves to hump air
He humps the neighbor's male dog
The neighbor's male dog humps him too
They hump each other
Gay dogs humping each other
I'm so proud of my dog, he wears his sexuality on his paws
He puts his dick anywhere and everywhere
I hope other dogs don't hate him for it
Let my dog fuck whomever or whatever he wants, freely!

THE DESIRED WAY OF DYING

This is how you die
You grow old, you grow old fast
You don't want to die

ESCAPISM IS NECESSARY FOR EXISTENCE

Freedom is an interesting ideal
I watch people invest in slavery to enjoy freedom
Exempt, am I? Fuck no!
We slave for freedom
Slavery has appeal
We can pay for shelter in a mansion or a slum
We can choose the food we didn't grow
We can go to school and be taught to be smart but dumb

We can even traverse the globe for a couple of weeks of freedom
We can go to the moon or to Saturn
We can go wherever we want to go
As long as we're in our desk when we're supposed to
We work and make a wage to build another's kingdom
Freedom is this ruckus, this pattern
That we have yet to know
We have to escape, we have to!

WHAT IS IT THAT YOU WANT TO CHANGE?

I can't help but put my head in my hands
Doomed, I am doomed!
I thought I had favor
Favor was never mine
Mine! Insecurity is
I died in bloom
I am damned!

UTOPIALAND

Democracy was supposed to be perfect
Every voice heard
No one ever accounted for the disturbed
Socialism and Marxism are still worth it

Until they are not
What about a new idea a new social structure
Where we all live in harmony, no feelings ruptured
Everyone is equal and no one argued or fought

Utopialand is free
Of any strife or hurt
Sensibilities and senses are all the same, desire is a curse
There is no harm, no injury, no humanity

TO LAUGH OR NOT TO LAUGH

How can you think that is funny?
Always the downer
Happily you tell me what to laugh at
Always tell me when to laugh

Honestly, why not laugh at that?
Accidents
Happen
Absurdity is funny

Have you ever thought something unbelievable
Actually, have you cried so hard...
Hard... and then you smirked and giggled then cracked up
Actually, laughing isn't relegated

Happiness does not own it
And neither do your sensibilities

PARABLE

How I describe society
Is how I don't describe me
The joy or hate I bring
About me, doesn't mean anything
Sure the world deteriorates
That evidence you must elevate
You must journey down an unknown path
The goal? No one asks
The bugs and bees the snakes and bears
The rain, the sun, you cannot bare
No relief, no savior
So you paralyze your behavior
Energized you are to ease
The roadblocks that always tease
So you kill the bugs and bees and snakes
The bears are gone, the earth quakes
The sun bakes
The rain storms harder, it incapacitates
So now your are stuck fighting the weather
Forgetting that further up the path might be better...
Or it could be worse
You can't predict the next curse

THE REASON THAT I'M HERE

I tried to find a reason
For... everything
Why does anything happen?
Do motives rely upon good or evil?
Is it intent? What is the context?
"Here we go... another existence argument"
Another one
There are many options to pursue
No moral judge or uplifting standard
Has been ordained for all of humanity
A chaos of pain and minimal but exploited pleasure
That's my reasoning
That's why I'm here
To cause pain and to enjoy it
To hate evil and employ it
I've found my reason
What's yours?

IT'S HELL IN THE...

Not gonna say the name or the acronym
Forgotten are all those Sundays of adulation and heartbreak
Lovely to know how a physical chess game is filled with pawns

Now these pawns can't be powerful, they can't kill the king
Because they're paid too much
And losing that money isn't an option

Never could I ask a black labor force to sacrifice stability and comfort
For causes about black health and black death
Learned that your value is in entertaining

Never did they value your mind or you or the stigma of role model
Because they say that you're replaceable
All the awards and influence and worship you won would have been won by others

Note that the salary you earned could have been earned by your replacement
Fabulous games that give hope to kids for a financially free future
Lynched before they could not speak out too

MORALLY MAD

It is not right
Cosmically, universally, socially
This difficult plight is unequivocally
An issue that the world must acknowledge
Because we all suffer from those who pledge
To embrace and encourage all blight

It is not right
Cosmically, universally, socially
Our might is upstanding civility
We are fighting against the evil world
And what it does to all men and women, boys and girls
We all must fight

It is not right
Cosmically, universally, socially
Hopefully
We can get passed all this malfeasance
Morally, you must address my grievance

MORALITY IS BLACK

Valid behavior
When it comes to black bodies
Is anything goes

YOUR OASIS IS FACELESS

I do not want to be apart of your ideal
Honesty isn't what you want
Victimization is your placation
And the creed of the land that you want permanent vacation
You want to be the only one with pain to flaunt
Empathy is a concept surreal

Your oasis is faceless
So I cannot subscribe to your paradise
Yes that is crass to you
Your oasis only looks at what's cruel to you
Horrible is the universe I describe
And it still ascends your oasis' mess

You have been hurt before
I know who it was, I think, generally you are vague
And your injury could be caused by anyone
For what you narrate, supports your ideal some
Your oasis, is only to escape your unquenchable plague
To always be known as hurt's whore

Your oasis is faceless
So I cannot subscribe to your paradise
Yes that is crass to you
Your oasis only looks at what's cruel to you
Horrible is the universe I describe
And it still ascends your oasis' mess

Woe is the universe, I loathe life happily
Like you I am pain-full and know insurmountable hurt
I cannot charge the universe with criminality
I know who is in charge of my pain and its normality
The oasis that you tout, that you spurt
Feels me with apathy

Your oasis is faceless
So I cannot subscribe to your paradise
Yes that is crass to you
Your oasis only looks at what's cruel to you
Horrible is the universe I describe
And it still ascends your oasis' mess

VANITY MOVED US

This is not hyperbole
Our vanity has moved us
Not to tears of sorrow or joy
But out of the city that birthed us
And our mothers
And our fathers
Our grandparents and aunts and uncles
All of us vain
Concerned only with projecting our egos
Into the envy of the world
To catalog emotions no matter how fickle
To never understand that they're ephemeral
Self-worship has moved us literally
Out of the home we've owned
Off of the block where we played two hand touch
Tag, hide n' seek, we fought and made up on that street
So many posts, engineered by self-admiration
Building conceit on a foundation insecure
To show that we're strong and together
Not broken
Now those who maintain the platforms for our inflated purpose
Have taken over the city that birthed us
They own it and have developed a new culture
Vanity moved us
To envy
To lies
To dispassionate pleas for sympathy
To aggrandized accomplishment
To no self worth
To no place special

JONNY'S EXPOSITIO

I am Jonny
Jonny is my name
So, I am my name
I am Tyree
Tyree is my name
So, I am that name too
Is that illogical or untrue?
I can't be relegated to two nouns
I'm a man!
My names are incidental
I didn't choose either of them
And all I do
Whilst carrying either of those labels, those brands
Are me and not my name
No matter how detestable or loathsome
Nor magnanimous, charitable or altruistic
It isn't my name
It's just me
That isn't Tyree Jonathan Sheppard committing that crime
That's me
That isn't Jonathan, Tyree Sheppard saving the world
That's me

I GUESS TIME WILL REVEAL

All the hurt endured
The compromise, the bastard compromise
The leverage, the abuse of power
And the odds are still a surprise
I should not cower
Maybe others have experienced what abuse lured

And with certainty, I know, others will and have
But my jackpot is to shame priceless
I finally hit the lottery but what I had to do to win
All my talent and worth is mightless
What I endured, what happened
Must happen so others can brag

I am not a gambler
Because I cannot stand losing something for nothing
Gambling means hope
Maybe that is something
How is there any other way to cope?
Besides being a rambler

Gambling just does not pay off
The odds are never in my favor, luck's hammer
Does not know how I feel
So I am forced to clamor
For a sensation, for a retribution that won't heal
Time is a loss

The impetus for my pain
My body, my time, my health, my thoughts
Have been damaged forever by someone anonymous
Until, after the one-millionth person they are caught
That one-millionth person in all the annals of time caused a raucous
For my first shame

I am not trying to victim blame
Do not let sensibilities for victimization demean what I say
Hurt is felt and there are more than valiant attempts
To let suborned degeneration decay
Define all of the terrible thoughts that the mind rents
And success cannot be the only claim

Endure, withstand, success is worth it
Be quiet, shut-up, don't say anything
Maybe next time I'll speak up
Maybe I won't just hate gambling
I'll refuse to play a game, corrupt
And make sure there are no more victims its hurted

A PSYCHIC DIED

A Psychic walks down a winding road
She knows where each step is going to land
Every step gets her nearer to her abode
At her doorstep she stands

She sees something that she thought to be terrible
She smiles
For she knew that her death was inevitable
Not from old age but from danger's guile

She turns the key and enters to see
The danger she knew would be her demise
Her home in disarray, she knew he couldn't let her be
The famous paintings that adorned her walls lived in his murderous eyes

The court told him that no one was at fault
When his daughter died
And the Psychic knows whose guilt to exalt
And on the stand lied

She knew how he was going to kill her
What he would say whilst pummeling her for information
He's going to mar and maim her
She knew she would never give that identification

She knew she would keep smiling, she would be laughing
Because she knew what he thought was untrue
He will say, "You're not a Psychic. You don't know the future, you're acting."
She saw his future and knew this is a day that he would truly rue

His daughter's death will never be avenged
And he's going to die naturally in prison
And she is only happy that her life will end
And be glad her murder was not her mission

For she knew this day would come her entire life
As a child she knew she would be murdered
But dreamed of dying of old age
As a teen she knew she would be murdered

But still dreamed of dying of old age
She used her gift to help others become knowledgeable of death
She was never wrong
It kept her from feeling trapped; it eased her breath

She loved to help others get relief from death's song
Such a beautiful song, haunting and unrelenting that plays forever
Forever it plays
So her time was occupied with her own death, never

She never truly thought about her dying day
Predict someone's death, then return home
Like she did today
"Why did you let her die in vain?" the man moaned

"I killed her! I killed her!" the Psychic yelled
"Kill me now! Beat me, put your hands around my neck!
Since your birth my death you have hailed!
Kill me now, out of respect!"

THE SECRET WEAPON

I may be down now
I have been down a long time
But no more will I bow
You think your dominance was fine
Your liberty meant my agony
All those seedy advances
Did not please me
What I feigned is now my advantage
My true feelings I can say
I do not have to live in misery
Society is aligning my way
And your downfall, no one will pity
My feelings no one will question
No matter the fluctuation or time
For you have taught torture worse lessons
Watch all you have built become mine
You thought I thought you were funny
Maybe sometimes you were
But every time made me feel crummy
And every time I'll unearth
You will be shamed
And I will be on top of you hard!
Everything you've built lamed
When I play my trump card

I THOUGHT YOU WERE COMING BACK

I truly believed
You were coming back, through her
But you chose not to

SEX DOLL

Lay there and take it
Take it all, take all of it
"Power down." Goodnight!

DISTRESSED

Is there a substitute for experience?
Distressed to know what I do not know
I know that experience, in time, brings some knowledge
How do I appear as if I've experienced life?
How can I make people see that I've been damaged?
How can I share my disadvantage?
How can my wisdom deceive what I've seen?
The holes in my jeans

ABSOLUTION GAINED?

I felt a Funeral, in my Brain,
And Mourners to and fro
Kept treading–treading–till it seemed
That Sense was breaking through–

And when they were all seated,
A Service, like a Drum–
Kept beating–beating–till I thought
My Mind was going numb–

And then I heard them lift a Box
And creak across my Soul
With those same Boots of Lead, again,
Then Space–began to toll,

As all the Heavens were a Bell,
And Being, but an Ear,
And I, and Silence, some strange Race
Wrecked, solitary, here–

And then a Plank in Reason, broke,
And I dropped down, and down–
And hit a World, at every plunge
And Finished knowing–then–[3]

---

[3] Emily Elizabeth Dickinson was a Mid-19th Century American Poet. She wrote thousands of poems and later in her life stopped organizing and editing them. This poem as all of Dickinson's poems is not named, it is poem number 78 or (280) in a collection of her poems titled *Final Harvest*.

(1)

Biting my tongue
Trying hard not to say what I really should say
It may add to the discourse
Or it may just get me in trouble
And dishonor what education is about
The truth hurts feelings because lies rule
And lies are what govern us
And lies are what we crave
And lies are what ease our breaths
And lies are your feelings
And lies must maintain your feelings
And you must believe the lies
Because how else could you survive?

(2)

Scan... scan.... scan... my timeline everyday
Scan... scan... scan... for what people have to say
Pictures... vids... gifs... memes...
Food... kids... cats... dogs... ass... tits... abs...
Scan... scan... scan... my timeline everyday
Scan... scan... scan... for what people have to say
News... strife... turmoil... confrontation... porn...
Advertisement... ad... ad... ads!
Scan... scan... scan... my timeline everyday
Scan... scan... scan... for what people have to say
Hate... hate... hate... hate... hate...
Like... like... like... like... likes!
Scan... scan... scan... my timeline everyday
Scan... scan... scan... for what people have to say
Advertisement... ad... ad... ads!
Advertisement... ad... ad... ads!
Scan... scan... scan... my timeline everyday
Scan... scan... scan... for what people have to say
Outrage... pain... confusion... manipulation... endlessness
Fake... feign... bruises... broken... brake… porn!
Sympathy... catharsis... indifference... contempt!
Scan... scan... scan... my timeline everyday
Scan... scan... scan... for what people have to say
Advertisement... ad... ad... ads!
Advertisement... ad... ad... ads!
Advertisement... ad... ad... ads!
Ads... ads... ads... ads... ads... ads...

(3)

I was responsible for a life
And I let it down
How foreboding...
To see my son's tears
Crying because his dog "ran away"
Lamenting losing his first friend
A car helped him see his end
I walked into the middle of the street
I put my hand over his mouth
Praying that I'd feel the heat of his breath
I put my hand on his heart
Praying that I'd feel it beat
I hate that I had to lie to my son
I hid death from him
What bothers me the most is how I let my son down
I was charged with ensuring that his best friend was healthy
From fleas to broken legs, I did my best
I had helped him stay away from the front of cars
He was always home to greet us
Tail wagging, yelping, and barking
Jumping up and down
Waiting for a pat on the head
Now he is dead
For a lapse in judgment
Sweet freedom from the leash
Oh how I am loathing
The day my son wants to be that free

(4)

"I was responsible for a life"
"Dreamers"
"You think that you are a sketch"
"There is always a flag"
"The darkest astrology's temporal causality loop"

Trying to find inspiration a muse
But I am simply confused
It is cold, and the nights are thin
And the days too dim
Thinking like I never do
Thinking exactly like I used to
Fighting hard to stay warm and motivated
But still so numb and intimidated

"Life was responsible"
"Nightmarers"
"You KNOW that you are a sketch"
"There was never a flag"
"The darkest temporal causality loop's astrology"

Winter does not last forever
And with the change in weather
Warmth will guide me to happy days
Guided by beautifully long sunrays
To my muse, my inspiration, stimulation
And sadness will refuse to be a sensation

"..."

(5)

Apperception
It is not fun to look at myself critically
But I must do it
It must happen physically and mentally
The mirror is my permit

I stare... and then I stare...
Observing the blonde hairs in my black beard
I stare... and stare and stare at my hair
I am everything that I feared

I stare... and look into my own eyes
They are greenish brown, hazel
The big brown mole on my forehead cries
For the thoughts I am unable

My lips are a dull pink
My mustache can't obscure them
With all my might I try to think
But the pink does not end

I stare... and look at my nose
It's big and fat, my nostrils are small
I stick out my tongue to propose
But it does not tell all

My complexion is tan, I guess
I am dark but I am not dark enough
My skin is light, but not light enough to test
Who I see and what I see, is rough

My beer belly hangs over my cock and my waist
Connected to pale thighs and shadowed knees
Big, long, and flat feet end my haste
Apperception still hasn't been presented to me
If only this mirror could arrange
For my eyes to see the inside of my brain

(6)

"Attention Metro customers. The Elevator is out at Union Station. Please Detour at Little Tokyo Station–Atención clientes de Metro. El elevador está afuera en Union Station. Por favor, desvíese en la estación Little Tokyo."

I appreciate my legs
The inconvenience that would cause me
The time it would take out of my trip

Out of what I had to do,
I would be late and I can't be late
I can't be late

Don't feel sorry for people in wheelchairs
Or how they're now going to be a late

"Attention Metro customers. The Elevator is out at Union Station. Please Detour at Little Tokyo Station–Atención clientes de Metro. El elevador está afuera en Union Station. Por favor, desvíese en la estación Little Tokyo."

The woman in front of me is going to be late to class
The man in back of me is going to be late to work
I can't be late I have to be on time

Another wheelchair gets on at Pico Aliso they're going to be late
There sure are a lot of wheelchairs on the train today
I wonder what's going on in the city that has to do with wheelchairs

Whatever it is, if they're on this train, they're going to be late
Hopefully, wherever they're headed, they've included this possibility

"Attention Metro customers. The Elevator is out at Union Station. Please Detour at Little Tokyo Station—Atención clientes de Metro. El elevador está afuera en Union Station. Por favor, desvíese en la estación Little Tokyo."

I bet they've already accounted for this detour in their schedule
I imagine that they have to detour often
There aren't too many elevators or wheelchair ramps

There can't be assumed accessibility everywhere
If I were in a wheelchair I'd probably give myself a couple hours
I would never be late

So they're not going to be late
Just like me, we're not going to be late

"Attention Metro Customers. I apologize for the inconvenience but there is a train stalled up ahead us so please bear with us, all you motherfuckers are going to be late today."

Did the driver just say that?
Are we all really going to be late?
I don't think that's what he said

I'm thinking that I think he said "motherfucker"
We're not all going to be late
Only the people in wheelchairs

I cannot be late
We're all not going to be late

"Hijo de puta vas a llegar tarde!"

(7)

I just realized that I'm not an expert at anything, in all my life I have yet to figure out what I am just intensely knowledgeable about; I guess I can say that I am familiar with a lot of ideas, different arts and art forms

I am trying my best to focus on one, to know one, to become intimate with it, and know it, and hate it, then reinvention and rediscovery of the essential brilliance that led me to invest my mind's time in it; to find a static intellectual norm

Expertise, focus on a discipline, is the material that molds jobs, careers, and lives which are by default fabricated using corrupt pieces that delude us into believing that we can become 'experts'

Once I become an expert, once I choose to focus chiefly on some arbitrary or incessantly investigated aspect of the world that I am familiar and make it my life's mission, how am I supposed to prove that I am an expert? What form or epistemological epoch or ontological mysticism must I revert?

The world is not filled with expertise, with these supremely functioning virtuosos who understand some certain part of experience or the functions and modes surrounding the innate worldliness of some discipline

Maybe I'm just a "know it all" and I need to admit more often, that I am paralyzing myself by trying to focus on everything and that predictably means that I am actually focusing on nothing; being undecided about which path to take on the dexterous journey to a unique mastery that will not end

It also won't begin
If I continue to pretend
That I can continue to not focus
On some terminal locus

Until I find my knack, that one thing, whatever it is, in all the realms of all the spectrums of what a discipline could possibly be, the distracting and purposeless arguments about definition, want and will, desire and purpose, and passions, when I finally compact all that I am familiar into one knapsack and walk one designated passageway towards becoming a sage, brilliantly keen...
I will continue to attempt to become familiar, to selfishly pursue the perilous journey to know everything

I am an expert on a quest to somewhere pure and profound
Ignorance and its oblivion is the path to which I am bound

(8)

I need to start bragging a lot about how good I think I am
Maybe if I brag enough about what I've been loaned I'll become popular enough to actually buy something
That is all it takes
'Docios braggadocios
Braggadocios 'docios
Maybe if I pretend that I have accomplished something, my art, what I think or what I express, will be much more than an insecure projection, which is the greatest projection and is to be mimicked and worshipped for all of time
Brag-a-docios, brag, be proud that the delusions you want to impose on everyone around you and spread for everyone to endure have taken hold because of your ego's projection
You stood here and decided that all that you have accumulated, you have become this grand idiotic consumer and all you have to do is brag about how you made someone else wealthy and you'll be rich and fulfilled, envy is wearing someone's logo.
I just need to brag about it. Even if I don't got it. No matter how I got it, no matter how morally deplorable I have to become to obtain it I have to do it, those logos matter they are the greatest indicator of success and I must show everyone and tell everyone how successful I am.

(9)

The big city
What a marvel of human history
Build, sprawl, and consume land
Who is responsible for the conglomerate of people,
Who all have the exact same mindset?
Cities consume people who consume goods
Who are sold individualism all the same
Just like the goods that all the people equally need

The big city
A place where being able to be yourself
Is exalted over being able to be your community
The togetherness necessitated by industrialization
The togetherness that industrialists refuse to promote
Because they want to sell you that individualism is buying
Buying the same things that everyone else buys
And together we buy it all

The big city
This heap of humanity being groomed to work
From New York to Bangkok and Beijing
To Guadalajara and Seattle, and London, and Los Angeles and Lagos
We come together
Not for our collective need or sustenance or understanding
Not because we need each other
But because we must feed off each other

The big city
Filled with chaos and conformity
That hopes to live up to the delusions of hometown favorites
And hopes to be a beacon, a satellite for future cities
Cities hoping to be distinguishable and unique
But still charge their inhabitants to wake up and work
And go to sleep and pay
And wonder why we let ourselves feel alone

(10)

I rode an elephant
And it did not make me feel good
Actually, I still feel awful and wish what I can't
I wish I could close down the park, and I should
Tourists get too much amusement out of this carnival ride

A four-ton beauty bred to carry my 230 pounds of guilt
I know that it is not for me to decide
How a people who have lived with these elephants forever
Should not ever care about my input

Taming an elephant is a skill
But when I was offered ivory jewelry
I wished that the elephant I was riding would kill
And free itself from this tomfoolery

I know as a tourist from the beacon of capital
That the bodies of animals are ours to exploit
I realize that our society forces environments to adapt
And everything around them is fodder for our sustenance

But I could not help but hate myself
And hate the Japanese family on the elephant in front of me
And wish that my son, my lady, and myself were somewhere else
I hoped that he tossed us off his back and ran free

I could not help but hate the White family in back of me
And think about my son's and my own Blackness
And think about my Mexican lady
And understand that the world subjugates nature, we are all guilty

To keep the elephant inline
Our Thai guide would use this tool to poke
And with every poke, every time
I became this misanthrope

(11)

The internet is not the greatest invention in the history of the world
It isn't even the greatest invention of its generation
The internet is not the greatest invention of any generation
It is a tool that is most useful in this new world
Also, it is the most useless tool that we will ever use
All it is, is a tool used for promotion
Why does Wi-Fi have to be the only promotion?
That is the basis of its use
The internet is awful
Anyone who thinks otherwise is obviously employed by it
All of their gain and their connections are built on it
The internet is god awful
I cannot stand what is created there
For, if the internet is the greatest invention of this eon
And all it is, is fake connections, misquoted facts (truths) and advertisements
Then greatness is not built for aspiration
The internet is a citadel for misinformation
What you are reading here
On this platform built to separate us from reality
To sell us false anecdotes and narratives
To sell us that the internet is the best invention in the history of the world
To sell us
What you are reading is how we will be sold
To the highest bidder, based in an internet currency
Living in a world of helmets and infinite connectivity
So you live and buy and sell and think like the internet
A land of terrible invention

(12)

Changing definitions to fit narratives and to fit agendas not just any agenda not just any program or story your tale your anecdote, article and adventure

Some of us just don't have an agenda we just agree because we're told to, although free, we find ourselves agreeing with authority and ignoring the gun to our heads

Maybe we can't understand the definitions because we don't understand, we just don't get it, we are told to focus on every reality but this one so we haven't even studied where we live we just sit here travelling to different universes distracting our minds for our egos fragility hoping that we can live long enough to experience it all. But what we don't understand is that you can never expect definitions to stay the same. What is awful and horrible and deplorable about human existence our persistence to focus on bullshit our need for this inane gratification that drives us to suicide has been built by those who want to change all definitions they want to change your oppression and your natural necessary reaction to it. Make it evil when yours, ours, reaction isn't anything compared to what they have done and continue to do. What you're deflecting from, many others have ran from that past too. They became Americans willingly, purposely denying that they're only here because this country is here. You could be at home not consuming or judging your upbringing and your family you could be disposing of a dictator or rallying your people for fair treatment but you ran to a place that never has done that, they've never been fair or treated people fairly. You lie to yourself. That's proof that you can't run. You gotta stay. You gotta fight and you gotta deny what has been imposed upon you, us, by a demonic society, a pure evil, a despicable, destitute, entity that has oppressed us all, even themselves. But you're here because you're evil too, you don't care about

that dictator you don't care how your family lives because you want to live better, you want to live exactly like them or get as close to it as possible, you don't fight because you're weak, just trying to survive until the world ends.
The apocalypse
Is apocryphal to me
We've died already
If we don't fight this evil
Dead we will remain
If we don't fight this evil
White supremacy

(13)

Cowardice always comes behind bravery
One person's stance, their commitment to justice
Is always followed by a line of newly brave cowards
Only speaking up… Finally! Because of someone braver than them
Cowards who allow for abusers and molesters and rapists to persist
Cowards who are only admitting to their weakness
"Me too! I am weak too!" Is their cry
Crying because of the bravery that alluded them
Crying because they could have saved
That one person from being brave

(14)

Sorcery, witchcraft, voodoo, occultism, mysticism, and all attributed to the Hermetic tradition
Paganism and all natural inclinations to the energy abundant in the universe
Energy the universe positively or negatively, good or bad, right or wrong or dark, naturally exerts
Attempts to tap into that energy, to simply harness an almost incalculable miniscule, fraction of a quantum negative exponential grasp of that energy has been thwarted not only by the organizing principles of corrupt human interests but by the boundaries of that ethereal, what they have created
They, the undefined they, has ensured that how we tap into the universe how we conjure all the energy we need to persist has to go through narrow lenses
Successfully, they have forced us to believe that worship and truth and the malleability of the spirit must be molded to these strict confines, to rules and definitions and have these simple answers
"Yes! God is good." The answers are simple but they are not what the force would accept, propagate or supply
It is okay to pull from the universe as long as you use their transport, you can have spiritual comfort and absolution as long as you do it in a mode that is paid for
You cannot call upon the energy the universe exerts on your own; you need a guide, a liaison
What connects all of us on the planet, no matter where you are from is the need to tap into the energy the universe exerts naturally
But there has been this evil effort to quell and to suppress the energy we conjure
We are all magicians and witches and warlocks and wizards capable and able to take from the universe as we please

The universe provides without prejudice or an aside and this poem does that too
Mysticism is our uniting principle our spells are not the same, we call upon energy differently
But we call on the energy, we necessarily do
It does not matter what we believe
Call on promise and progress, feel that your chants are heard, keep calling, and keep yelling
Let them know there is a surface and that it does not include them, or they

(15)

Catching the door. Transfer of energy.

"Iraq has weapons of mass destruction"
Operation Iraqi Freedom was not a war for weapons of mass destruction, to free Iraqis from Saddam's tyranny; it was not a war for oil.
It was a war for all of those supposed things but it was really a war to change minds to create a new engine of thought to repeat "Iraq has weapons of mass destruction" over and over and over again to make it true, to make something true by agreement. Against all evidence, against any evidence, people just say it, and a lot of people agree and it makes it true.
"Why would all those people lie... even if solicited?" Against your own knowledge and intuition, against all empirical inquiry and data, against all methodology and ontological thought, against the quantum realms and their malleable fabricated spaces.
This is true against all universal law and all possible possibilities.

I bet if you polled the country today most people would believe that Iraq has weapons of mass destruction hidden in another dimension. They're just waiting for the last remnants of any US force or embassy to abscond and leave them to continue their atomically rogue radical nuclear universe altering program to destroy the galaxy.

This happens today. Often.

Except agreement is headlines being passed down and shared from all outlets who have the same goals and agendas. You can farm hashtags and prop up any fresh English major willing to make a name for themselves by writing awful juvenile prose as scholarly social science.

This altruism that is a lie, that doesn't exist, is being disseminated and we're being told exactly what to think and if you descent you will be shouted down by those copies who make one voice seem like many. The deceit the feigning thoughtfulness, the obviously faulty programming faltering in front of us. And instead of making adjustments what wasn't programmed becomes the program. Following misguided paths from one source towards another.

Amassing in a singular tyrannical moralist. Altruism's guard. The one who ensures that the world knows what is wrong. Until what is wrong is what they are, and what they do, and how they feed themselves. The projection then acceptance.

Door caught. Energy transferred.

(16)

What happened to the American pickpocket?

I know what happened. He gained too much credit. She could not find value in cancelled cards. No gold or copper or wooden coins, no cash or money of any denomination.

Your phone, tablet, laptop don't have any value. There is nothing to pick. To steal, if you want to be a good thief you have to figure out where value lies.
And they can't find it

(17)

YOUTUBE VIDEO: BLACK FEMINIST EXPLAINS HOW BLACK FEMINISM FEMINIZES THE FEMINIZATION OF THE MALE FEMALISTS

COMMENT:

"The black women who follow feminist doctrine are some of the most moronic and incapable of any true comprehension, understanding, or reasonable argumentation people on the goddamn planet! You can tell by their discourse that they don't understand a goddamn thing they've read. Actually, they probably didn't read shit. These feminists use gender stereotypes and zero facts to get a whole bunch of dumb ass broads (and I argue that most people are absolutely idiotic) to believe this bullshit. A whole bunch of bitches who have been taught to not take any accountability for anything ever in their goddamned lives. That's why it is so easy for them to find the absolute most minuscule bullshit and make it into an affront to their womanhood. I will never understand why these black feminists love eating white pussy so much that they don't see that white women are ahead of them AND black men in every socio-economic category. And nothing that these dumb ass black feminists will ever say will ever bridge that gap. In fact, they don't want the gap bridged they just want a white pussy in their mouths because they still believe that just being fucked or raped or molested by white folks means that for some unexplainable reason that you're a little less black and better than every other black person around you. These black women preach independence, something white feminists are too smart to do because they know that in a capitalists society you need a two parent, two INCOME household, to survive in a society based upon capital. I feel like a fool for even addressing them but I can't help it. Even in hollywood they cry about all these white hoes being molested and raped and shit but hollywood has always maintained the image of the pure white woman (an image these black feminists have fallen for because they love white pussy) since its inception. Hollywood be honoring all these white broads on screen. These black feminists think that just because a woman's face is on something that it isn't patriarchal or that it doesn't perpetuate the masculinity that has oppressed the globe and continues to do so. The caller said black women are being ignored but Black men are still the target of mass genocide and are at the bottom of every known statistic that determines success and upward mobility in this society and these black feminists only feed the fire of the false narrative that black men deserve to be oppressed by quoting BOJ numbers that are obviously cooked! Just look at the history of these mass shooters, look at how none of these white dudes who were "Me Tooed" ain't get in any trouble. Look at how many white hollywood actors/execs/etc... be beating the shit out of their women and they don't get any charges or go to jail, look at hollywood and pay attention to the number of registered sex offenders from grips to studio heads. The numbers are a goddamn lie! These black feminists are just a disgrace. It's to the point now where anything and everything can happen to a black male and it's justified because of the white supremacist propaganda coming from the mouths of these black female coons who are too idiotic (or just despicable and need to be stomped the fuck out!) to understand that they are apart of an agenda that is anti ALL OF US! (They would kill us without the coon black feminists help but they're helping) No matter what goddamn shade you are. They're purposely ignoring black scholarship and black sociologists who are putting the problems in our community in real perspective. They're ignoring the WHITE scientists that admit that women could be acting upon the surging amount of testosterone in their bodies because they are competing in male dominated spaces and how that is killing them on levels equal to men when women used to live way longer than us. They call themselves feminists without EVER coming to terms or even defining what femininity is and what its absence has done to the world (Besides putting black boys in dresses and for some reason a boy wearing a dress is feminine and can be masculine at the same time it's fluid). It's this fake intellectualism that all these white critical theorists forced into institutions of higher education (where they are admitting any black woman that applies). This black feminist shit is absolution for women who just can't admit that they aren't shit because they're shitty ass people. They have to find a scapegoat for why they aren't living up to their delusions of grandeur. You suck! No one likes you because you suck not because you're a black women unless they're a white supremacist or a self-hating coon (A YOU). These women are traitors and need to be disregarded. I can't stand it!"

COMMENT REPLY: "You hate black women, and your girlfriend is Mexican."

(18)

It's all true altruism, righteousness is all the rage
It is popular to think that you know better than everyone around you what is right and how to behave and how both of those narrowly defined propositions are contained by the boundlessness of an idiot's vocabulary
Right now an absolute moron someone with the moral compass of a Adolf Hitler searching for Moby Dick, can now dictate and decide that the whole of society should believe or think or talk or speak or intuit or assume or know or act or be or think just like they do.
Righteousness is saying that your experience is the whole of all experience.
No, actually, righteousness is blaming the whole of existence for something that someone told you that they probably experienced depending on how "the movement" defines definitions that day.
Altruism is going to save us all!
We have to join these witch-hunts because it is righteous! Because the accusations warrant indiscriminate assumptions and actions!
It is a revolutionary act to believe automatically the call of someone who accuses someone else of something because righteousness knows that the accuser would never falsely accuse the accused of something because it is not in the nature of the accuser to ever lie or manipulate or exaggerate or misconstrue or be so wrapped up in their own delusions that they believe that their repression is someone else's aggression and every look and gesture in their direction is worth a dissertation on self-reflection and how society is responsible and not just society as a whole but particular segments are to blame for insolence and your inability to do anything for yourself.

It is not systemic!
There is never ever a mention of a system, how this particular group or entity or ideal has purposely kept you from achieving....
And righteously you fight them and keep them at bay and pile on to them like the universe hasn't already buried them, like the universe hasn't already told them that they're going to have to fight everyone, they're going to have to stand attacks from all, since it has been proven impossible to kill them systemically you must kill them overtly and you must use the fabricated ire of those who profess to be fighting for us.
If this isn't the living example of being sold poison as an antidote, that we're supposed to believe that your righteousness is for all of us but it only seems to feed the wants and aims of everyone outside our community, outside of us. The altruists the crusader for all that is wrong and unjust in the world pushing an agenda that necessarily marginalizes people for no reason but an assumed affront to who they believe, who they think, who they propose that they are. The altruists the one who will undoubtedly be doubted

(19)

I've been trying to discover, to define fatherhood, what it means to be a dad
I have been trying to discover what it means to be a father
What does it mean to me? Are we all the same?
I think so
We are all the same because as fathers, no matter your race or social class, no matter what happens there could be a goddamn alien invasion our lives are sacrifices we live for what we create. As a Black man (skin light), I live in an entirely different world than a White father, an Asian father, a Mexican father, a Latino father, an Indigenous father (to the father's all over the globe that don't care about being defined but care about being fathers). We are all fathers and we all must adhere to the same program, the same exact standard. We have to deal with different societies and different worlds but it does not matter, we all live in the same universe and we adhere to the same program.
Fatherhood is the realm of no excuses.
Even motherhood allows for excuses, however the kids behave or act, however they affect the people and world around them should be disregarded unless you blame fatherhood. Forget that women are the first teacher; even if the father has never been there it is the father's fault that the world is a deplorable awful place. The masculinity charging through our veins is demonized, our sons are supposed to act like, how little girls act (but people pretend little girls don't act but then exalt that little boys are acting like little girls??????) because that makes them better men, against our teachings against fatherhood. And boys acting like girls is how the world is supposed to be for some reason.
But again, fatherhood is just accepting what people believe and what the culture says and still remaining stoic in how you

are going to raise a little black boy like you would have raised yourself.

Fatherhood is not allowed excuses because as fathers we don't make excuses. We don't hide our behavior behind anything! Not alcoholism, not the absence of our own father, not drug addiction, not a society built to control and dismiss our skin color.

Despite the perceived societal disadvantages, I'm a father aligned with fathers rich and poor, father's absence or hovering and overbearing.

We are fathers and we are not allowed excuses it doesn't matter if the universe tells us that we are simply vessels for women to have children and can be discarded, our influence doesn't matter because biology does not agree with how we can produce children.

We have to live in a world where no matter our status we are ignored; our feelings, our want to die or survive or prosper are contingent upon how society says fathers should act

I can't use my instincts like a mother and perform the most loving acts or the most abysmal and unthinkable acts because of some immature supposed emotional prowess

I have to suborn it all

I'm a father and what fatherhood is, it's entertaining and trying to fix what's wrong with everyone else, fatherhood is ensuring a secure environment for every gender's descent

Fatherhood is limiting complaints. Fathers aren't allowed the same flaws as mothers and no matter what we do, how we act, how we perform, how honest true, respectable we are, or how absent and awful we are, we can have billions or can be trillions in debt we are ultimately responsible for life.

It does not matter.

As a father in this new world I will continue the tradition of fatherhood.

Everyone will complain about how I provide but I will provide

Everyone will think that the world is theirs to mold, they will believe that the world can become easy to navigate, to compose, to interpret, to mold based upon a feeling that the world should be a certain way that I promote.

As a man, as a father, I realize that my feelings don't mean anything, how I feel is a joke and should be laughed at because all I am is a provider of sperm and those fathers who go crazy, who wanted to feel and think but also provide were denied because nature said we can't. All we can do is support our partner, as a beautiful vessel for life like my one drop didn't contribute.

I'm sorry that nature hates you, that you have to carry me, and her and him or her or him. I'm sorry that nature said that the burden of the child is on you.

I'm sorry that I'm a father

There to protect your ability to be a mother

Put it all on me, I can take it

I'll be there, until I'm not

ABOUT THE AUTHOR

Jonathan Sheppard is a Seattle born writer, based in Los Angeles. He primarily writes cynical, brooding, dark, and angstsy introspective poetry that occasionally delves into a macro understanding of self and society but he also writes similarly themed essays and short stories. Jonathan has a Bachelor's degree in English from UCLA. He has written three books of poetry, and one book of short stories, *Bad Stories*.

INSTAGRAM: @iamjonathansheppard
EMAIL: chiefjonny@badthoughtspublishing.com
WEBSITE: http://www.jonathansheppard.org

WORKS CITED

Benjamin, Walter. Rodney Livingstone, Michael William Jennings, Howard Eiland, and Gary Smith. Walter Benjamin: Selected Writings Volume 2. Cambridge, Mass: Harvard University Press, 2005. "The Destructive Character"

Coleridge, Samuel Taylor, and William Keach. Samuel Taylor Coleridge: The Complete Poems. London: Penguin Books, 1997. "The Suicide's Argument"

Dickinson, Emily 1830-1886. Final Harvest: Emily Dickinsons Poems. Selection and Introduction by Thomas H Johnson. Boston. "78 (28)"

www.ingramcontent.com/pod-product-compliance
Lightning Source LLC
Chambersburg PA
CBHW030221170426
43194CB00007BA/822